Hexagrams

Anna Blackmer

Fomite
Burlington, VT

Copyright 2019 © Anna Blackmer
Cover: Anna Blackmer and Andy Sacher
Author Photo: Andy Sacher

All rights reserved. No part of this book may be reproduced in any form or by any means without the prior written consent of the publisher, except in the case of brief quotations used in reviews and certain other noncommercial uses permitted by copyright law.
ISBN-13: 978-1-944388-49-2
Library of Congress Control Number: 2018941380
Fomite
58 Peru Street
Burlington, VT 05401
www.fomitepress.com

Hexagrams

Contents

Part I

The Gentle (The Penetrating, Wind)	2
Before Completion	4
The Arousing (Shock, Thunder)	6
The Marrying Maiden	8
Coming to Meet	10
The Corners of the Mouth (Providing Nourishment)	12
Dispersion (Dissolution)	14
The Clinging, Fire	16
Splitting Apart	18
The Wanderer	20
Return (The Turning Point)	22
The Well	24
Duration	26
The Taming Power of the Small	28
The Family (The Clan)	30
The Abysmal (Water)	32
Decrease	34
Increase	36
Possession in Great Measure	38
Standstill (Stagnation)	40

Part II

Influence (Wooing)	44
Waiting (Nourishment)	46
Conflict	48
Youthful Folly	50
Darkening of the Light	52
Revolution (Molting)	54
Following	56

Gathering Together (Massing)	58
Modesty	60
The Taming Power of the Great	62
Work on What Has Been Spoiled (Decay)	64
Limitation	66
Preponderance of the Small	68
Preponderance of the Great	70
Fellowship with Men	72

Part III

Approach	76
Break-through (Resoluteness)	78
Abundance (Fullness)	80
The Cauldron	82
Treading (Conduct)	84
Keeping Still, Mountain	86
Contemplation (View)	88
Inner Truth	90
Retreat	92
Progress	94
The Army	96
Holding Together (Union)	98
Difficulty at the Beginning	100
Peace	102
Pushing Upward	104
Enthusiasm	106
Oppression (Exhaustion)	108
Grace	110
The Power of the Great	112
Opposition	114
Biting Through	116
The Receptive	118
Innocence (The Unexpected)	120

Development (Gradual Progress)	122
Obstruction	124
Deliverance	126
After Completion	128
The Creative	130
The Joyous, Lake	132
Author's Note	135
Sources	138

The Gentle (The Penetrating, Wind)

The wind never stops blowing
and you lose your dark glasses in the lagoon.
Now you can see the dark corners of the room,
the corners of the eyes of the houseboy
who crouches under the table.
The wind blows through you so that he might see it.

The wind blows through you so that he might see it.
Is that you crouching under the table,
cornered by the eyes of the houseboy?
You can see the corners of the room,
now that you've lost your dark glasses in the lagoon.
The wind never stops blowing.

Before Completion

The unending wall of preparation
ceases to glow at twilight, and you find yourself
alone on the ice. Young thing, think again,
remember how you left your house—
full of guests, the ghostly kettle
boiling on the cracked enamel stove.

The kettle, full of ghosts, boils
on the cracked enamel stove.
Remember how you left the house—the guests all gone.
Young thing, you're alone and on the ice, so think again;
cease to glow at twilight, and you'll find yourself
near an unending wall of preparation.

The Arousing (Shock, Thunder)

Shocks come in two from below.
After years, you leave one life in an evening
and laugh with another 'til the sun comes up.
It's raining, and your heart rises
from the womb to its proper place, caged,
for all to see, all fear to travel to.

So all can see it, fear travels
from the caged womb to its proper place.
It's raining, and your heart rises,
laughs with another 'til the sun comes up.
After years, you leave your life in an evening.
Shocks come in two from below.

The Marrying Maiden

Across the lake, you see the end of the world.
No one was with you in the beginning,
no one led you to this beach.
But here he is! Waiting in his long, green boat,
ready to stare at the other shore with you
as he rows across the joyous water.

Once he rowed across the joyous water,
ready to stare at the other shore without you.
But here he is! Waiting in his long, green boat.
No one led you to this beach,
no one was with you in the beginning.
Across the lake, you see the end of the world.

Coming to Meet

Still, some young girl lives on inside your body,
avoiding your legs, your unbound feet.
Sometimes her breath comes to meet you,
wafting like a ripe melon from heaven.
Will your old self turn to her,
knowing the scent of imminent death?

Knowing the scent of imminent death,
will your old self turn to her,
sensing a ripe melon from heaven?
Sometimes her breath comes to meet you,
avoiding your legs, your unbound feet:
that young girl who lives on inside your body.

The Corners of the Mouth (Providing Nourishment)

For months he dreamt of fish. Mornings he talked,
evenings you served each fish to him
like an accusation. Then his mouth seemed to close,
there beside the frozen harbor, his words
only lamps providing light for those old folks
who built their houses on the ice to drill for food.

Who built their houses on the ice to drill for food?
Only lamps provided light for those old folks,
there beside the frozen harbor. Each word you spoke
was like an accusation, and then his mouth seemed to close.
Evenings you served the fish to him,
and for months he dreamt of them. Mornings he talked.

Dispersion (Dissolution)

It was music broke the ice.
We might be thankful for the sacrifice, those
floes which mark a path over livid, un-invented water,
creating sight, jabbing your heart as if to break…
cold cupidity, that boyish statue, melts
into a song not even meant for you.

The song wasn't even meant for you.
Cold cupidity, that boyish statue, melts,
creating sight, jabbing your heart as if it could break up
those floes which mark a path over livid, un-invented water.
We might be thankful for the sacrifice:
it was music broke the ice.

The Clinging, Fire

Making bright sores, you hold the past in your hand,
a lump of coal burning itself up.
It was once alive, a surprise
of smashed fronds just learning this art of dependence.
Look, the stars cling to time
in a heaven which clings to nothing.

In a heaven which clings to nothing,
look at this: the stars cling to time.
The past was once a surprise of smashed fronds
just learning this art of dependence.
Now it's a live lump of coal burning itself up.
Making bright sores, you hold the story in your hand.

Splitting Apart

You cut the headlights and comb the darkness
with your fingers. Over your shoulder,
the driveway, twisted and pale, is a remnant.
The keys are implements for going in,
the bed a twin, a mirror, a disappointment.
Its dreams couple in the empty room.

Dreams couple in the empty room;
the bed's a twin, a mirror, a disappointment.
The keys are implements for going in—
the driveway, twisted and pale, looks like a remnant
over your shoulder. You cut the headlights
and comb the darkness with your fingers.

The Wanderer

So leave the house. It was a destination
you sat in and never reached. The neighbors' windows
are solid gold rectangles, and the moon
blinks on and off like a sign.
Give up what you can see in the dark—
luck draws you to the mountain and the ache of the view.

So luck draws you to the mountain, and then the ache of the view.
If you give up what you can see in the dark,
there's the moon blinking on and off like a sign,
and the neighbors' windows are the solid gold rectangles
you desired and never reached.
Leave the house. It was only a destination.

Return (The Turning Point)

In a world where silence means perfect order,
the seasons change in a day. So the old men were right:
if you turn the chair away from him,
you can say anything. The words are familiar.
Place your hands above the new lamp
and call the gesture devotion.

He called the gesture devotion
when you placed your hands above that new lamp.
You can say anything to him; the words
are unfamiliar only if you turn the chair away.
The seasons change in a day, and the old men were right:
it's a world where silence means perfect order.

The Well

It will always be here.
The townspeople walk beneath canopies of trees,
listening for the faint sounds of water.
You had seen their vague movements as simply allegory
or stupidity, and you were wrong.
We need each other, and tie bucket to pole.

We needed each other, and tied bucket to pole.
Or to stupidity: you were wrong because
you had seen their vague movements as simple allegory.
Listening for the faint sounds of water,
the townspeople walk beneath canopies of trees.
Will they always be here?

Duration

Which moment would last forever?
Windpipe, sacrament: you said yes before
and no after he did. Marriage
is just a clue, an atmosphere—
your words are sparks never
to be extinguished, only forgiven.

Never extinguished, spoken only to be forgiven,
your words are sparks.
Marriage is just a clue, an atmosphere:
you said yes before and no after he did.
Windpipe, sacrament, moment.
Which one would last forever?

The Taming Power of the Small

Someone said your hands were beautiful—
secretly pleasing, and confusing to have hands
at all in this world made of wind, sky,
and unbreakable evil. You're always looking
down at them, folded palms-up, thinking
of the small things you once did to please him.

Thinking of the small things you once did to please him,
you're always looking down at your hands,
folded palms up. In this world made of wind, sky,
and unbreakable evil, it's confusing
to have hands at all. But you're secretly pleased:
someone said they were beautiful.

The Family (The Clan)

They say it's up to the woman. Correct, correct,
and correct. The fire burns brightly
until the wind dies—you have to force yourselves
to keep talking about the same things.
Outside, crickets rub their legs against the night,
and the cats are leaping and feasting.

The cats are leaping and feasting outside,
and crickets rub their legs against the night.
Keep talking about the same things
until the wind dies—you have to force yourselves
to correct. The fire burns brightly:
they say it's up to the woman. Correct, correct.

The Abysmal (Water)

You want to tell him you know:
desire runs downhill like water
your hands are hidden under.
But your ignorance is also vast
and wet. You're touched by his innocence
as he swims just above you.

As he swims just above you, all wet,
you're touched by his innocence,
but your ignorance is also vast.
Now your hands are hidden under his desire—
it runs downhill like water.
You want to tell him you know.

Decrease

The twist of paper in your hand
becoming torque and rope ascending.
The tree, tree with no children in it,
where you go to let the branches bend
and hold you. What was lost?
Was it money in your lonely fist?

Was there money in your lonely fist?
The branches bend and hold you. What
was lost when you climbed into that tree,
tree with no children in it,
becoming torque and rope ascending?
A twist of paper in your hand.

Increase

The music is wind, and the thunder
down there the sound of cars colliding.
Almost everything has been replaced
by fear sizzling in its bowls.
But don't worry—they're full—and *don't*
means *will* in that place of scattered offerings.

Don't means *will* in that place of scattered offerings.
But don't worry—you're full
of the fear sizzling in those bowls.
Almost everything has been replaced:
down there, the sound of cars colliding
is music, is wind, is thunder....

Possession in Great Measure

As the sun goes down, people begin to walk
toward him across the fields, swinging their arms
and legs with pleasure. He builds a fire
in the center of the new foundation, to bless it,
before he aims at heaven, while his drunken guests
pass food around beneath the muted stars.

His drunken guests pass food around beneath the muted stars
before he aims blessings at heaven
from the center of the new foundation.
He builds a fire and lags with pleasure.
Swinging their arms as the sun goes down,
people begin to walk across the field, away from him.

Standstill (Stagnation)

The cold edges of the mountains ruffle
against the retreating sky. You're inside
the little white car, trying to get home, trying
to keep your eyes on the black heavens, on your daughters,
on your sister, as they move away. Be still,
for *all things are benumbed* until grass is parted from sod.

All things are benumbed until grass is parted from sod.
Gaze on your daughters, on your sister, as they move away—
be still, keep your eyes on the black heavens
from inside the little white car, try to get home
against the oncoming sky. Know you're as cold
as the ruffled edges of the mountains.

Influence (Wooing)

Are you wooing me, mister?
Or is the sketch just mountainous angles and pencil dust?
Someone has to be still, but I've gone all soft
resting in the curvature of your eyes.
You surprised me, out here beyond the age of influence,
out there where happiness has lived all along.

Out there where happiness has lived all along
you surprised me: I'm beyond the age of influence,
resting in the curvature of your eyes.
Someone has to be still, but I've gone all soft—
or is the sketch just mountainous angles and pencil dust?
Are you wooing me, mister?

Waiting (Nourishment)

It took just a month—an eternity in a dumb rush,
the brush of wing over sternum—
to make me wait, to understand I'm starving.
Compression, then ease on the borders of sorrow.
The table is loaded with meat and wine and pie.
The moment I sit down, I know I can't have it.

The moment I sit down, I know I can't have it,
though the table is loaded with meat and wine and pie.
Compression, then ease on the borders of sorrow.
I had to wait to understand I'm starving,
like the brush of a wing over sternum.
It took just a month—this eternity's a dumb rush.

Conflict

After dinner I sulked and sat on the porch
smoking and watching the lake go one way,
the stars another. I could feel the peptides flatten,
remember a year of tearing sounds inside my body.
And those dreams! First this side of the hall, then that;
it wasn't love, either, behind each door I opened.

It wasn't love, either way, behind each door I opened.
And those dreams! First this side of the hall, then that;
I remember a year of tearing sounds inside my body;
I could feel the peptides flatten, as I smoked and watched
the lake go one way, the stars another.
After dinner I sulked and sat on the porch.

Youthful Folly

Teacher, teacher…as the water fell, I fell—
all over each other to get down the mountain—
and the still moment of recognition was wasted.
On youth, of course, its metallic sweetness
an incision in the side of innocence, its innocence
a spring filling up those cracks, cushioning the abyss.

A spring fills up those cracks, cushioning the abyss,
an incision in the side of innocence, that innocence
youth, of course. Its metallic sweetness
and the still moment of recognition were wasted.
We were all over each other, to get down the mountain—
teacher, teacher—as the water fell, I fell.

Darkening of the Light

Driving up Route 36, one headlight gone,
the other flickering, I watched the full moon rise
over Bellevue Hill, white as an aspirin
on the day before my period.
His body once covered me, blotting out
everything I no longer wanted.

Everything I wanted no longer blots me out;
once, his body covered what I could see
of the full moon in the days before my period.
Over Bellevue Hill, I watched it rise,
white as an aspirin, one headlight gone
as I drove up Route 36, the other flickering.

Revolution (Molting)

I'm losing—some fur, feathers, or those silky shirts
you sent last Christmas. My ancestors peer
from the pages of the calendar at my nakedness,
counsel no regret with their softened, impersonal eyes
in spite of the burning deep within the lake. This turning hurts,
this marking days and boundaries out.

This turning hurts, this marking days and boundaries out,
in spite of what softens deep within the lake.
My ancestors counseled no regret, peering at my nakedness
with their burning, impersonal eyes
from the pages of the calendar you sent last Christmas.
I'm losing—some fur, some feathers, those silky shirts.

Following

I wanted both the boy and man, but the one I followed
for years left only a little electricity
bathing in the lake over the long, solitary winter.
And as the standard changes, the yoke becomes permanent:
the horse still pulls his cart across the heavens each day;
the ox ploughs circles around our house-for-sale.

The ox ploughs circles around our house-for-sale;
the horse still pulls his cart across the heavens each day.
As the standard changes, the yoke becomes permanent:
only a little electricity left bathing in the lake
over the long, solitary winter. For years I wanted both
boy and man, but not the one I followed.

Gathering Together (Massing)

Outside the house, someone called out, someone
laughed, someone sighed. I missed the party
again, and my whole life began to gather
above me with its floods of tears
and secret messages corked up in the wine bottles
I'd emptied during my difficult and crowded youth.

I'd emptied myself during a difficult youth
crowded with secret messages corked up in wine bottles.
Above me, flooded with tears again,
my whole life began to gather.
Someone laughed, someone sighed. I missed the party.
Outside the house, someone called out.

Modesty

Tonight the hooligans are riding around in cars,
limiting themselves to three kinds of squash—
whatever will explode the brittle windows
on my street that stare like shocked citizens
who've only meant to keep their eyes modestly averted,
their radiance aimed to pools on the sidewalks below.

Our radiance aimed to pool on the sidewalks below,
we only mean to keep our eyes modestly averted.
But on my street tonight, we stare like shocked citizens
at whatever might explode our brittle windows.
Limiting themselves to three kinds of squash,
the hooligans are riding around in cars.

The Taming Power of the Great

I only meant to hold myself together—evaporate
what little pain I felt—the sentences fluttering out of the past,
the poets of antiquity rolling their eyes at my lack of manners:
"She feeds herself in a different restaurant every night!"
Meanwhile, back at the office, the male animal is tied tightly
to a stake in the ground and the sun unmerciful.

A stake is driven into the ground and the sun's unmerciful.
Meanwhile, back at the office, the male animal smiles tightly:
"She feeds herself in a different restaurant every night!"
The poets of antiquity roll their eyes at my lack of manners,
at what little pain I seem to feel—their sentences fluttering out of the past.
I only mean to hold myself together—or else evaporate.

Work on What Has Been Spoiled (Decay)

The wind blows around my ankles—almost too far away
to see from up here in the frozen neurotic
where my shoulders never stop aching. What will it be:
habit or despair or the wide-open gate
and a bowl of worms? They say it was spoiled
by the mommy—so be extra kind in the fixing.

Spoiled by the mommy—so I was extra kind in the fixing.
And the bowl of worms? They say it meant either habit
or despair or the wide-open gate.
My shoulders never stop aching. What will it be?
Almost too far from up here in the frozen neurotic
to see where the wind blows around my ankles.

Limitation

There's more water in the sky than in the lake.
More money in heaven than in the bank.
You sat in the booth drinking rum and looked at me
without measuring from here to there.
I was laughing like a fool—well, wasn't I a free spirit?
Hadn't I learned what looking and looking could do?

Haven't I learned what looking and looking can do?
I was laughing like a fool—well, wasn't I a free spirit?
Without measuring from here to there,
you sat in the booth drinking rum, looking right at me.
But tonight there's more money in heaven than in the bank,
more water in the sky than in the lake.

Preponderance of the Small

How was it brought to my attention, that bird flying
too high, too fast, and straight toward the very thing I wanted?
Or maybe not....The mountains seem claustrophobic
and the weather is lousy—my life wedged
behind the bureau like the necklace slipped out of my hand,
and can only be retrieved with patience and a stick.

It could only be retrieved with patience and a stick,
there behind the bureau like the necklace that slipped out of my hands.
And the weather is lousy—my life wedged just so.
Or maybe not.... The mountains seem claustrophobic:
I was flying too high, too fast, and straight toward the very thing I'd wanted.
How was it brought to my attention, that bird?

Preponderance of the Great

If the big tree falls, it should land smack on the ridgepole
of the house. Was that where we all slept once,
as the foundation silted further south and the walls bowed out?
But the heavy machines move forward—one can never keep up
with the newspapers, or even the furniture ads. I was flowering
underwater, like a poplar, growing and rotting at the same time.

I was flowering underwater, like a poplar, growing and rotting
at the same time, along with the newspapers and furniture ads.
But the heavy machines moved forward—one can never keep up—
as the foundations silted further south and the walls of the house
bowed out. Was that where we all slept once?
If the big tree falls, it should land smack on the ridgepole.

Fellowship with Men

I was looking for something when I went to the island
with a violent past. I saw fish in water the color
of heaven and cane fires that distorted the fields at night.
I didn't need to stand on top of the wall that had absorbed
the blood those crowds demanded just after the revolution.
There was a gate, and I walked through it to join the others.

There was a gate, and I walked through it to join the others
the crowds demanded just after the revolution. I didn't need
to stand on top of the wall that had absorbed their blood.
Cane fires distorted the fields as the night passed,
and I saw fish in the water—a violence of heavenly color—
something like what I was looking for when I came to this island.

Approach

Where were the people? The bluff still overlooking the lake,
the prams empty along the promenade, the many boats, like smiles,
blowing in to shore. It should have been a time of greatness,
that's what I read, the leader standing off to the side,
the bureaucrat bending, bending, and the mouths all counted.
You could feel the New Year exhale, already behind you.

You could feel the New Year exhale, already behind you,
the bureaucrats bending and the mouths all counted.
That's what I read, the leader stands off to the side, his smiles
blowing in to shore. It should have been a time of greatness,
but where were the people? The prams empty along the promenade,
the many boats. The bluff still overlooks the lake.

Break-through (Resoluteness)

A river, my body, overflows its banks, the edges
of the clouds unfurl, whipping the blue where I think
I can see people jumping out of a building that's not on fire.
There is unease in the city. *We know things we can't touch*.
Draw a line, maybe leave town on your birthday.
This age, hesitation can be dead.

This age, hesitation can mean death.
Draw a line, maybe leave town on your birthday.
There is unease in the city. *We know things we can't touch*.
I can see people jumping out of a building that's not on fire.
Clouds unfurl, whipping the blue where I think a river,
my body, overflows its banks, its edges….

Abundance (Fullness)

The greedy close their curtains at noon to see stars
and avoid the beggars. So as not to worry,
I spent all my money in about a minute.
Now I want to share everything with you.
Too late, the sun is priceless, enigmatic,
a shy god vamping as a big ball of gases.

A shy god vamps as a big ball of gases—
but we're too late, and the sun is priceless, enigmatic.
I wanted to share everything with you,
though I spent all my money in about a minute
and now avoid the beggars. So as not to worry,
the greedy close their curtains at noon to see stars.

The Cauldron

What came out of the pot fed us,
consolidating our linked fates, the jade handles
of the vessel glowing even under those harsh fluorescents.
And if a concubine's womb is turned over,
what happens to the son—oh, god—
what happens to the daughter?

So what happens to the daughter?
What happens to the son—oh god....
If a concubine's womb is turned over,
the vessel glows even under those harsh fluorescents,
consolidating our linked fates. The handles were jade:
what came out of the pot fed us.

Treading (Conduct)

They said he let her walk all over him
(I was eating chocolate and plucking at his coat
as if he were my long lost father).
The harbor lights meant speaking carefully as you watched
each lie snuff out, meant not being caught looking
and talking at the same time.

We were talking at the same time:
each lie snuffed out meant not being caught looking.
The harbor lights meant speaking carefully as you watched
(as if he were my long lost father,
I was eating chocolate and plucking at his coat).
They said he let her walk all over him.

Keeping Still, Mountain

Happy New Year (and be quiet). No shoes allowed
in the zendo, stop slumping, the bell ringing
a hundred times in the courtyard, a single eye in the room opening,
opening. Later she burns all her bills in the fireplace.
The dust is counted. He has a problem with authority.
So what can be coming when we sit so still in the night?

What can be coming when we sit so still
in the night? He has a problem with authority.
Later she burns all her bills in the fireplace. The dust is counted
a hundred times in the courtyard, a single eye in the room opening,
opening. Stop slumping in the zendo. The bell rings
happy New Year (and be quiet!). No shoes allowed.

Contemplation (View)

The dent in the wall grins back at me—like looking
in a mirror where your image fades and reappears. The others
are quieting, and one leaves her body behind and steps outside.
The snow looks like raw fiberglass on the cars in the parking lot,
and there's a tower, far away in China, written with ink,
watching through the years to where she stands.

I'm watching through the years to where she stands
beside a tower, far away in China, written with ink.
The snow looks like raw fiberglass on the cars in the parking lot.
The others are quieting, and you leave your body and step outside
into a mirror where your image fades and reappears.
The dent in the wall grins back at me—like looking....

Inner Truth

We were thick as thieves once, but intractable one to the other:
him being pig-headed and me cold and dumb as a fish.
You had yourselves a nest—oh, empty egg!
And a pretty little river meandering around the property.
The wind played on its surface—played, I say—and the rippling
took it all away. Gently, brutally, all along….

And the rippling took it all away. Gently, brutally, true
all along, the wind played on its surface—played, I say—
and a pretty little river meandered around the property.
You once had yourselves a nest—oh, empty egg!
But him being pig-headed, and me cold and dumb as a fish,
we were thick as thieves, intractable, one to the other.

Retreat

The mountain rises to its full height—is it a hill of beans,
a tower of abandoned cars, or a monument to the captains of industry
and their faithful servants? And how, exactly, do we get away?
You were singing to me of the ether, that blue place so thin
I might never need a coat or a new pair of shoes again, where
there was plenty of company and an idea of what to do.

There was plenty of company and no idea of what to do.
I might never need a coat or a new pair of shoes again, in that blue place
so thin you were singing to me of the ether and our faithful servants.
And how, exactly, do we get away from that tower
of abandoned cars or the monument to the captains of industry?
The mountain rises to its full height—a hill of beans.

Progress

Was he honking his horn in celebration or to punish the city?
After the polls closed we counted the ballots—everyone
voted for the same person—and as the sun rose I saw
hundreds of horses being led along the main drag. The buildings
looked pink as hope, now that the bars had all been closed.
Now that people could sleep.

Now that people could sleep the buildings looked pink
as hope; now that the bars had all been closed,
hundreds of horses were led along the main drag.
Everyone voted for the same person—and as the sun rose I saw
the polls had closed, and we counted the ballots.
Was he honking his horn in celebration or to punish the city?

The Army

Spring's coming, and the wagons are filled with multitudes—
whether they're dead or alive is up to interpretation—and whose
scimitar is the moon tonight? Whose animals strip the fields?
Like everyone, you look for the person in charge—I want to know
the rules at least, the force that fills the earth with water
and holds it there until it breaks.

At least the rules hold it there until it breaks,
that force that fills the earth with water.
Like everyone, you look for the person in charge—I want to know
whose scimitar is the moon tonight? Whose animals strip the fields?
Whether they're dead or alive is up to interpretation.
Spring's coming, and the wagons are filled with multitudes.

Holding Together (Union)

After months the rain finally comes and comes
and won't stop. My table is small, the garden
drowning by the meadow, and danger waits on the sand,
under the mud. Do we only do what we know to?
In the pit, many cups of tea help him avoid scandal
in the faces of his uninvited guests.

In the face of uninvited guests,
many cups of tea help him avoid a scandal in the pit.
Under the mud, do we only do what we know to?
The garden's drowning by the meadow, danger waits on the sand
and won't stop. My table is small;
after months the rain finally comes and comes.

Difficulty at the Beginning

The warehouse was already full, and we'd just begun to try
to love again. "They warn you in the first fifteen minutes,"
she had said, and I realized there was nothing to do
but empty it and watch the deer jump into the clouds
that hid the forest. You see, I lived in that world for years,
packing and cleaning and freezing and beginning anew.

Packing and cleaning and freezing and beginning anew—
that hid the forest. "You see, I lived in his world for years,
but emptied it and watched the deer jump into the clouds,"
she had said. And I realized there was nothing to do
to love again. They warn you in the first fifteen minutes.
The warehouse was full, and we'd just begun to cry.

Peace

At the start of the year the cliques of ass-kissers fell apart—
what was small held its place in the center of my heart
as the borders were flung open so we could remember
where they were. While the super-rich spent their money
on endless light, in that other hemisphere someone pulled
up ribbongrass, and I came along with the roots.

Someone pulled up ribbongrass, and I came along with the roots
and the endless light of that other hemisphere.
Where were we while the super-rich spent our money?
The borders were flung open so we could remember,
and what was small held its place in the center of my heart.
At the start of the year the cliques of ass-kissers fell apart.

Pushing Upward

The light moves north and the wind comes racketing in
so hard from the south that the neighbors' American flag
turns stiff above the melting snow. It seems effortless,
the way the maple trees have grown up in the center
of the empty city. The sun is dragging us closer,
out of our dark beds, up and away from each other.

Up and out of our dark beds, away from each other
and the empty city. The sun is dragging us closer,
as the maple trees grow up the center,
turning stiff above the snow. Melting seems effortless,
blowing hard from the south into the neighbors' American flag.
The light moves north, and the wind comes racketing in.

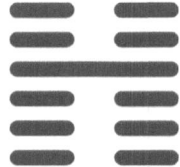

Enthusiasm

You went to the museum and saw yourselves as precursors
of delight—dancing together at last in the films and maps
of the past. Someone jumped around as a building
was torn down in fast motion. History breaks my heart,
humbles me coming to the end of my own, the drums calling,
calling out the ancestors from their hiding places.

The drums calling, calling out the ancestors from their hiding place
humble me coming to the end of my own.
As a building is torn down in fast motion, history breaks
my heart of the past. Someone jumps around
in delight. Dancing together at last in the films and maps,
you went to the museum and saw yourselves as precursors.

Oppression (Exhaustion)

She lived in the mouth of her job, perplexed
at what she had or hadn't been able to do with words
and why nobody was paying attention. Only it was me,
tired and stuffed full of plums, knees the color of fruit
just fallen from the tree. Maybe I'd been holding on to rancor,
mistaking it for joy coming softly over the exhausted lake.

She mistook it for joy, just fallen from the tree,
coming softly over the exhausted lake. Maybe she'd been holding on
to rancor, tired and stuffed full of plums, knees the color of fruit.
Why was nobody paying attention? Only it was me,
and what I had or hadn't been able to do with words.
I lived in the mouth of her job, perplexed.

Grace

Their bonfire, meant to take in what was cast away,
lit up the stillness and made it beautiful. But that was not
the point. By yielding, I gave you form, if only
for a moment—your brocades weren't meant
to last—though you saw truth as an adornment,
and I was who I was in my long white dress.

I was who I was in my long white dress, and though you saw
truth as an adornment, your brocades weren't meant to last.
By yielding, if only for a moment,
I gave you form. But that was not the point.
The bonfire lit up the stillness and made it beautiful,
meaning to take in what was cast away.

The Power of the Great

I think he meant to say *Sweetheart, can you hear me?*
but I was working on my muscles at the gym and wasn't listening.
The body politic—we're as entangled as the goat in the hedgerow—
can inch neither forward nor back and twisting makes it worse.
Power moves toward heaven and leaves us to choose, knowing
we long for the strong one to guard where we live in our skulls.

We long for the strong one to guard where we live in our skulls.
Power moves toward heaven and leaves us to choose, knowing
we can inch neither forward nor back and twisting makes it worse.
As for the body politic—we're as entangled as the goat in the hedgerow.
But I was working on my muscles at the gym and wasn't listening.
I think he meant to say *Sweetheart, can you hear me?*

Opposition

I saw myself on the opposite shore of the lake, watching
the sun rise over rock, pine, and that back alley where you
dutifully meet your boss at dawn. What comes after the family?
Daughters like arrows that fly around corners.
Shorter days, elaborate dinners and medical procedures, a spill of wine
from the cup of an old adversary moving at you across the table.

A spill of wine from the cup of an old adversary moving at you
across the table, shorter days, elaborate dinners and medical procedures.
Daughters like arrows that fly around corners
where you dutifully meet your boss at dawn. What comes after the family?
Watching the sun rise over rock, pine, and that back alley,
I saw myself on the opposite shore of the lake.

Biting Through

She would not listen, and didn't, and didn't straddle
the mountain during the hardest part of the afternoon:
you know, the moment when punishments are meted out, just
after the thunder sidles past the paper shredder and rolls down the hall.
On the screen you could barely see that
his tigers were full of arrows.

His tigers were full of arrows.
On the screen you could barely see them,
as the thunder sidled past the paper shredder and rolled down the hall.
You know, the moment when punishments are meted out:
just straddle the mountain during the hardest part of the afternoon.
She would not listen, and didn't and didn't.

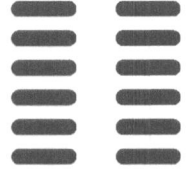

The Receptive

It appears that you can't even count—I mean,
who's keeping track? How many wild geese flew over the house
this spring, last fall? Maybe the answer lies with the inner life:
surely the rain would fit, and there's even a dry plateau, high up,
where you can wander around like a mare who grazes
incessantly, looking for the brilliant moment.

Like a mare who grazes incessantly, I'm looking for the brilliant
moment when you can simply wander around in the spring.
Surely the rain would fit, and there's even a dry plateau, high up.
Maybe the answer lies with the inner life, but who's keeping track?
I mean, how many wild geese flew over the house last fall?
It appears you can't even count.

Innocence (The Unexpected)

She thought her breath might be taken away
unexpectedly, like a cow tethered too long in the short grass
by the side of the road or that woman who just walked off
the job into a thunderstorm. After vertigo
I lay in the dark whispering in anticipation: no and no and not me;
this time I will finish what I started.

This time I will finish what I started.
After vertigo I lay in the dark whispering: no
and no and not me, anticipating a thunderstorm
by the side of the road. That woman just walked off the job
unexpectedly, like a cow tethered too long in the short grass.
She thought her breath might be taken away.

Development (Gradual Progress)

Is it a swan or a wild goose or a girl? No matter,
you must always start at the shore and mix your metaphors.
The plateau is where armies meet and the river
widens toward the sea. But they keep moving
according to ritual: cliff, plain, tree, summit, cloud.
Things cannot stop forever.

Things cannot stop forever.
They keep moving according to ritual: cliff, plain, tree,
summit, cloud. But the place the river widens
toward the sea is the plateau where armies meet.
You must always start at the shore and mix your metaphors.
Is it a swan or a wild goose or a girl? No matter.

Obstruction

He's gone lame, suddenly, off-kilter and leaning on his walker;
she's got bundles of grass stored in the attic.
Not much room to come and go, or go and go:
we all come to this place, our backs against the mountain.
I tried to tell them the rising water was dangerous, right out
front, to stay home with friends.

I tried to tell them, right out front, to stay home
with friends, that the rising water was dangerous.
We all come to this place, our backs against the mountain.
Not much room to come and go, or go and go:
she's got bundles of grass stored in the attic;
he's gone lame, suddenly, off-kilter and leaning on his walker.

Deliverance

I came back from the southwest, flying over the fires
and prairies, into the bursting green of home.
Then a thunderstorm a day until she was forgiven,
until her shame dissolved into ordinary shame,
held in the long yellow arms of the lightning.
Dark harmony between sisters, okay, maybe deep water.

Dark harmony between sisters, okay, maybe deep water.
held in the long yellow arms of the lightning.
Until her shame dissolved into ordinary shame,
then a thunderstorm a day until I was forgiven.
Into the bursting green of home she came, back
from the southwest, flying over the burning prairies.

After Completion

Just finished with dinner, that's when there's nothing left
and we walk down to the river. Time to cross over,
time to swim with your tail in the air, to stuff the veil
into the cracks of the leaky boat, to become suddenly humble.
No big hurry. She called out to me over the water,
You don't need that baggage to come aboard....

I didn't need all that baggage to come aboard....
No big hurry, she called out to me over the water
and into the cracks of the leaky boat. To become suddenly
humble, to stuff the veil and and walk down to the river,
to swim with your tail in the air. Time for us to cross over:
just finished with dinner, when there's nothing left.

The Creative

The angel's wings were red, and all the elements were there:
the man, the woman, the tree in flames, the up-cast eyes.
It went as predicted—at first I wrote because I loved him
and then I just wrote until the dizzying light evaporated
into the shortest night of the year. It was easy,
the sun was everything in this northern heaven-on-earth.

The sun was everything in this northern heaven-on-earth.
It was easy: I just wrote until the dizzying light evaporated
into the shortest night of the year. And it went as predicted—
at first I wrote because I loved him, and then I saw the man,
the woman, the tree in flames, the up-cast eyes.
The angel's wings were red, and all the elements were there.

The Joyous, Lake

Two mouths, two lakes, and four brother islands to the west,
out where the sun hits the water. A jet ski cuts the moment in half,
and there are screams of delight all up and down the shore.
What emptiness fills up here? What joy?
The lake replenishes itself in conversation—
and all of us join in, practical, foolish, all of us.

All of us join in, practical, foolish, all of us,
while the lake replenishes itself in conversation.
What emptiness fills up here? What joy?
There are screams of delight all up and down the shore,
just where the sun hits the water. A jet ski cuts the moment in half:
two mouths, two lakes, and four brother islands to the west.

Author's Note

These poems were written over a period of more than 30 years, so they form, in some sense, an autobiography. I wrote the first few simply as a way to engage with the great Chinese book of divination and cosmology, the *I Ching,* or *Book of Changes.* I was trying to slow myself down and write through something "outside" myself. I used the Wilhelm/Baynes translation, at the time the only one widely available to a layperson like myself. I never felt, during the entire time I was writing these poems, like approaching the text as a scholar—in fact, I resisted my own half-hearted attempts to do that, as well as the Jungian commentaries that I found. In time I became more aware of the irony that I was writing from a translation of a translation, but by then, I couldn't stop.

The I Ching has been used for thousands of years as a book of philosophy, ethics, good government, and divination—and according to Eliot Weinberger, in "China and in East Asia, it has been by far the most consulted of all books, in the belief that it can explain everything." Many scholars believe it originated sometime before 1600 BCE, and its history is a mixture of myth and academic conjecture. Fu Xi, a legendary figure, not completely human, who also was reputed to have invented cooking, is credited as having come up with the eight trigrams that are the basis for the whole "system," each composed of three stacked solid or broken lines (solid or broken referred to either yang or yin). These trigrams represented earth, mountain, water, wind, heaven, fire, thunder, and lake—a distillation of the cosmos. Later, King Wen, who founded the Zhou dynasty, doubled the trigrams and named each of the 64 hexagrams that now comprise the book. Subsequent contributors—the Duke of Chou, King Wen's son, as well as Confucius—added text, more commentary, social and moral categories, as well as images that linked ideas and more elemental realities.

What I came to love about reading the I Ching, and the process of using the text as a springboard for poems, was that I felt as if I were living in its images; though they were images that had arisen out of a time and culture I didn't know, they were very much alive and still had an almost spooky resonance for me (and millions of others, of course). And they spoke of a world-view that, though more meticulously organized than the rubble of the 20th and 21st centuries, was familiar in that it was rife with tensions between flux and order, darkness and light, rawness and refinement. The texts were deeply serious and simultaneously wacky in the way they resisted single interpretations.

I was also steeped in Modernism and its fascination with chance operations. I was enamored with the Dadas and Marcel Duchamp, and had seen a John Cage performance at the Sanders Theater at Harvard in the mid-1970's that used and referenced the I Ching—it was exhilarating, chaotic, at times beautiful, at times boring or incomprehensible. Someone in the audience I later recognized as a friend shouted out: "Take it back to New York!" But the paradox of using chance operations as a way to write about my emotions, my own life, intrigued me. It also scared me a little, which I liked (though what one "liked" or "felt" was anathema to Cage and most other late moderns).

I made a number of arbitrary and naïve choices about form and approach. I titled each poem with the name of the hexagram, using titles in the Baynes/Wilhelm translation. I struggled with pronouns—the youthful self-consciousness of the reflexive "you," the nakedness of the first person—and finally began to slide them around in the third section. The poems were composed as I consulted the I Ching, and ordered themselves chronologically. Most critically, I started out writing 6-line poems, and ended up writing 12-line poems. One "reads" the hexagrams of the I Ching from bottom to top, and each line has a different relationship to each of the other lines, as well as to the "situation" in general. The way one consults the oracle, using either yarrow stalks or coins, can also create "changing" lines, which sometimes results in different interpretations of the hexagram and even a change into a new hexagram. I began to compose the doubled hexagram poems knowing that I would reverse the order of the lines, though I wrote more in the spirit of curiosity than of calculation—by then, certainly, these poems were leading me away from myself, from what I already knew.

Sources

All titles are taken from Richard Wilhelm's translation of *The I Ching or Book of Changes*, rendered into English by Cary F. Baynes.

Fomite

About Fomite

A fomite is a medium capable of transmitting infectious organisms from one individual to another.

"The activity of art is based on the capacity of people to be infected by the feelings of others." Tolstoy, *What Is Art?*

Writing a review on Amazon, Good Reads, Shelfari, Library Thing or other social media sites for readers will help the progress of independent publishing. To submit a review, go to the book page on any of the sites and follow the links for reviews. Books from independent presses rely on reader to reader communications.

For more information or to order any of our books, visit
http://www.fomitepress.com/

More Titles from Fomite...

Novels
Joshua Amses — *During This, Our Nadir*
Joshua Amses — *Ghatsr*
Joshua Amses — *Raven or Crow*
Joshua Amses — *The Moment Before an Injury*
Jaysinh Birjepatel — *Nothing Beside Remains*
Jaysinh Birjepatel — *The Good Muslim of Jackson Heights*
David Brizer — *Victor Rand*
Paula Closson Buck — *Summer on the Cold War Planet*
Dan Chodorkoff — *Loisaida*
David Adams Cleveland — *Time's Betrayal*
Jaimee Wriston Colbert — *Vanishing Acts*
Roger Coleman — *Skywreck Afternoons*
Marc Estrin — *Hyde*
Marc Estrin — *Kafka's Roach*
Marc Estrin — *Speckled Vanities*
Zdravka Evtimova — *In the Town of Joy and Peace*
Zdravka Evtimova — *Sinfonia Bulgarica*
Daniel Forbes — *Derail This Train Wreck*
Greg Guma — *Dons of Time*
Richard Hawley — *The Three Lives of Jonathan Force*
Lamar Herrin — *Father Figure*
Michael Horner — *Damage Control*
Ron Jacobs — *All the Sinners Saints*
Ron Jacobs — *Short Order Frame Up*
Ron Jacobs — *The Co-conspirator's Tale*
Scott Archer Jones — *And Throw Away the Skins*
Scott Archer Jones — *A Rising Tide of People Swept Away*

Fomite

Julie Justicz — *Degrees of Difficulty*
Maggie Kast — *A Free Unsullied Land*
Darrell Kastin — *Shadowboxing with Bukowski*
Coleen Kearon — *#triggerwarning*
Coleen Kearon — *Feminist on Fire*
Jan English Leary — *Thicker Than Blood*
Diane Lefer — *Confessions of a Carnivore*
Rob Lenihan — *Born Speaking Lies*
Douglas Milliken — *Our Shadow's Voice*
Colin Mitchell — *Roadman*
Ilan Mochari — *Zinsky the Obscure*
Peter Nash — *Parsimony*
Peter Nash — *The Perfection of Things*
George Ovitt — *Stillpoint*
George Ovitt — *Tribunal*
Gregory Papadoyiannis — *The Baby Jazz*
Pelham — *The Walking Poor*
Andy Potok — *My Father's Keeper*
Frederick Ramey — *Comes A Time*
Joseph Rathgeber — *Mixedbloods*
Kathryn Roberts — *Companion Plants*
Robert Rosenberg — *Isles of the Blind*
Fred Russell — *Rafi's World*
Ron Savage — *Voyeur in Tangier*
David Schein — *The Adoption*
Lynn Sloan — *Principles of Navigation*
L.E. Smith — *The Consequence of Gesture*
L.E. Smith — *Travers' Inferno*
L.E. Smith — *Untimely RIPped*
Bob Sommer — *A Great Fullness*
Tom Walker — *A Day in the Life*
Susan V. Weiss — *My God, What Have We Done?*
Peter M. Wheelwright — *As It Is On Earth*
Suzie Wizowaty — *The Return of Jason Green*

Poetry
Anna Blackmer — *Hexagrams*
Antonello Borra — *Alfabestiario*
Antonello Borra — *AlphaBetaBestiaro*
Antonello Borra — *Fabbrica delle idee/The Factory of Ideas*
L. Brown — *Loopholes*
Sue D. Burton — *Little Steel*
David Cavanagh — *Cycling in Plato's Cave*
James Connolly — *Picking Up the Bodies*
Greg Delanty — *Loosestrife*
Mason Drukman — *Drawing on Life*

Fomite

J. C. Ellefson — *Foreign Tales of Exemplum and Woe*
Tina Escaja/Mark Eisner — *Caida Libre/Free Fall*
Anna Faktorovich — *Improvisational Arguments*
Barry Goldensohn — *Snake in the Spine, Wolf in the Heart*
Barry Goldensohn — *The Hundred Yard Dash Man*
Barry Goldensohn — *The Listener Aspires to the Condition of Music*
R. L. Green — *When You Remember Deir Yassin*
Gail Holst-Warhaft — *Lucky Country*
Raymond Luczak — *A Babble of Objects*
Kate Magill — *Roadworthy Creature, Roadworthy Craft*
Tony Magistrale — *Entanglements*
Gary Mesick — *General Discharge*
Andreas Nolte — *Mascha: The Poems of Mascha Kaléko*
Sherry Olson — *Four-Way Stop*
Brett Ortler — *Lessons of the Dead*
Aristea Papalexandrou/Philip Ramp — *Μας προσπερνά/It's Overtaking Us*
Janice Miller Potter — *Meanwell*
Janice Miller Potter — *Thoreau's Umbrella*
Philip Ramp — *The Melancholy of a Life as the Joy of Living It Slowly Chills*
Joseph D. Reich — *A Case Study of Werewolves*
Joseph D. Reich — *Connecting the Dots to Shangrila*
Joseph D. Reich — *The Derivation of Cowboys and Indians*
Joseph D. Reich — *The Hole That Runs Through Utopia*
Joseph D. Reich — *The Housing Market*
Kenneth Rosen and Richard Wilson — *Gomorrah*
Fred Rosenblum — *Vietnumb*
David Schein — *My Murder and Other Local News*
Harold Schweizer — *Miriam's Book*
Scott T. Starbuck — *Carbonfish Blues*
Scott T. Starbuck — *Hawk on Wire*
Scott T. Starbuck — *Industrial Oz*
Seth Steinzor — *Among the Lost*
Seth Steinzor — *To Join the Lost*
Susan Thomas — *In the Sadness Museum*
Susan Thomas — *The Empty Notebook Interrogates Itself*
Paolo Valesio/Todd Portnowitz — *La Mezzanotte di Spoleto/Midnight in Spoleto*
Sharon Webster — *Everyone Lives Here*
Tony Whedon — *The Tres Riches Heures*
Tony Whedon — *The Falkland Quartet*
Claire Zoghb — *Dispatches from Everest*

Stories
Jay Boyer — *Flight*
L. M Brown — *Treading the Uneven Road*
Michael Cocchiarale — *Here Is Ware*
Michael Cocchiarale — *Still Time*

Fomite

Neil Connelly — *In the Wake of Our Vows*
Catherine Zobal Dent — *Unfinished Stories of Girls*
Zdravka Evtimova —*Carts and Other Stories*
John Michael Flynn — *Off to the Next Wherever*
Derek Furr — *Semitones*
Derek Furr — *Suite for Three Voices*
Elizabeth Genovise — *Where There Are Two or More*
Andrei Guriuanu — *Body of Work*
Zeke Jarvis — *In A Family Way*
Arya Jenkins — *Blue Songs in an Open Key*
Jan English Leary — *Skating on the Vertical*
Marjorie Maddox — *What She Was Saying*
William Marquess — *Boom-shacka-lacka*
Gary Miller — *Museum of the Americas*
Jennifer Anne Moses — *Visiting Hours*
Martin Ott — *Interrogations*
Christopher Peterson — *Amoebic Simulacra*
Jack Pulaski — *Love's Labours*
Charles Rafferty — *Saturday Night at Magellan's*
Ron Savage — *What We Do For Love*
Fred Skolnik— *Americans and Other Stories*
Lynn Sloan — *This Far Is Not Far Enough*
L.E. Smith — *Views Cost Extra*
Caitlin Hamilton Summie — *To Lay To Rest Our Ghosts*
Susan Thomas — *Among Angelic Orders*
Tom Walker — *Signed Confessions*
Silas Dent Zobal — *The Inconvenience of the Wings*

Odd Birds
William Benton — *Eye Contact: Writing on Art*
Micheal Breiner — *the way none of this happened*
J. C. Ellefson — *Under the Influence: Shouting Out to Walt*
David Ross Gunn — *Cautionary Chronicles*
Andrei Guriuanu and Teknari — *The Darkest City*
Gail Holst-Warhaft — *The Fall of Athens*
Roger Lebovitz — *A Guide to the Western Slopes and the Outlying Area*
Roger Lebovitz — *Twenty-two Instructions for Near Survival*
dug Nap— *Artsy Fartsy*
Delia Bell Robinson — *A Shirtwaist Story*
Peter Schumann — *Belligerent & Not So Belligerent Slogans from the Possibilitarian Arsenal*
Peter Schumann — *Bread & Sentences*
Peter Schumann — *Charlotte Salomon*
Peter Schumann — *Faust 3*
Peter Schumann — *Planet Kasper, Volumes One and Two*
Peter Schumann — *We*

Fomite

Plays
Stephen Goldberg — *Screwed and Other Plays*
Michele Markarian — *Unborn Children of America*

Essays
Robert Sommer — *Losing Francis: Essays on the Wars at Home*

www.ingramcontent.com/pod-product-compliance
Lightning Source LLC
Chambersburg PA
CBHW030117100526
44591CB00009B/430